The Gift

by

Lila Ellexson Senter

DORRANCE PUBLISHING CO., INC.
PITTSBURGH, PENNSYLVANIA 15222

RoseDog Books
701 Smithfield Street
Pittsburgh, PA 15222
Visit our website at *www.dorrancebookstore.com*

ISBN: 978-1-4349-1088-2
eISBN: 978-1-4349-5938-6

Dedication

To Hope and All Hope Angels

It takes so many to bring a project to fruition, and many have provided the fruits for this book, *The Gift*. Through your contributions, each of you is a gift, and each of you has given a gift, multiplying the love and joy of this undertaking.

May the book itself convey our thanks to all involved: encouragers, creators, underwriters, experts in the field, marketers, contributors, beautiful friends, and precious family—all who share the Gift of Hope.

Lila Senter

Berries In The Snow by Barbara Nicholson

Christmas Word Gifts From Lila Senter
Enriched by these Artists and Photographers:

Hannah Capra
Nancy Capra
Sarabeth Clevenger
Carie Hampton
Ruth Jackson
Sydney Senter McKinney
Jane Milstead
Maggy Morford
Linda Johnson Murphy
Tootsie Nichols
Barbara Nicholson
Marinda Robertson
Billye Proctor Shaw
Tril Stratton
Rosemary Suttle
Ginger Womack Taylor
Alice Wright
Bill Wright
H.C. Zachry — Cover

Cosmic Angel by Sarabeth Clevenger

Introduction

Welcome to this small book—a medley of "word gifts," one given each Christmas for the last twenty-seven years. You might wonder, "What is a word gift?" For me, it is a very particular choice of words especially chosen for a special person or special persons. These particular words may touch another heart or soul through humor, pathos, fellowship, common interests, and a variety of other forums. It is one more way to reach out, to connect.

A word gift can be as brief as a quote, a poem or prose, a short story, a legend from another source shared and referenced by you, or original words from your head and heart. They are used for a variety of occasions: weddings, births, birthdays, bereavement, anniversaries, thank-yous, congratulations, or "just because." For whatever means or for whatever reasons you choose to share a word gift, it is your way of saying, "I am thinking especially of you."

I would delight in saying this was my original idea, but it was not. Returning to college to complete the education that marriage and children had interrupted (no, no regrets), I was so fortunate to have not only my husband, Bill, but an exceptional professor who encouraged me on this path. The professor's name was Caroline Couch Blair of McMurry University. One day in class, she presented us with a "Word Present." This elicited an excited reaction from me! It was a lovely moment. Enchanted with the magic of words since childhood, she had indeed given us a unique and wondrous gift.

That moment must have remained in my heart and thoughts for a long time, for several years later at Christmas, as I wondered how we could touch our friends in a more personal way than typical cards, the idea sprang to mind: a word gift! So the seed, planted and dormant for so long, burst forth and became characteristic of many of my notes ever since.

My poetry in this book is just part of a long endeavor of writing for pleasure; I certainly never thought of putting anything into a book. Yet a combination of events did come together the last few years: friends' affirmation and encouragement to do so; and my dream of an endowment begun for Hope Haven. Could this possibly work? To work, it must be more than a book of words. How about words enhanced by friends' art and photography? Would they be open to such an idea? You see the answer on the cover page; how graciously and generously they each shared their uniquely wonderful talents.

And unto one he gave 5 talents, to another two, and to another one; to every man according to his several ability.
Matthew 25:15

Having then gifts differing according to the grace that is given to us...
Romans 12:6

Now there are diversities of gifts, but the same Spirit...
1 Corinthians 12:4

The Heavenly Host Sings Praises by Sarabeth Clevenger

Foreword:

Gifts

My gift was recognized for the first time by a fourth-grade teacher. The children in her room sat in double desks, where we passed notes and shared secrets easily with our desk partners. The problems of the world were beyond our perspective, but we were happy learners.

In the back of our room, however, sat a boy several years older than the rest of us. He had severe learning problems. At that time, there were no special-education classes, and the boy sat isolated by his handicap, not taking part or expecting to take part. I don't recall being touched by his loneliness, but my teacher decided to water the seed of my gift so it could grow. She asked me to stay in and talk to her, then asked me if I would let Charles share my double desk, help him, and try to include him in recess activities. I said I would.

This was a deep assignment for a little girl, but my teacher had somehow sensed the gift inside of me which needed to grow, and the next day Charles was moved up front with me.

I remember how bad his tennis shoes smelled. He was slow at learning, but I tried to teach him. I would take him by the hand to include him in recess games and choose him to be on my side in spelling bees, knowing he would cost points. I was learning something more valuable than "readin', writin', and 'rithmetic." I was learning how much fun it was to give without the motive of receiving. I was also learning how important Charles really was. Although I did not perceive it at the time, the wisdom of this teacher and the experience she put in motion changed my life and pointed it in the direction that God had intended all along.

A gift! Thank you, God, for giving me the gift to recognize the tears behind the mask of another human being, for giving me the desire to do something about them, and for giving me the ultimate joy of your love when I do. What better gift could be given? God does not call the equipped, but He equips the called. What a beautiful gift, to be entrusted with the treasure of what God loves the most—the people He created. And although our missions are accomplished in different ways, and our journeys are in different directions along different paths, each is the gift He has given us all.

Years gave practice to my gift, and in February of 1992, my son, a medical doctor, suggested we try to do something about the homeless situation in Abilene, Texas. Our first vision was to find a condemned house, repair it, and turn on the utilities so people could find shelter in extreme weather. What a mess that would have been! But God took our vision, turned it into His vision, and led us mightily in His direction. Soon a building was given, the City Council gave backing, and the Abilene Association of Congregations, comprised of representatives from twenty-three local churches, gave its blessing and sponsored the project. A board of directors was appointed, a name adopted, and the idea of Hope Haven was born!

The city produced a host of volunteers, and donations poured our way from other churches, clubs, schools, and individuals. In June 1993, Hope Haven opened its doors to its first recipient: a young mother and her two-year-old daughter who had been born in a vacant warehouse. The mother had been on the streets since the age of thirteen, but she was now tired of drugs and insecurity and wanted a better life for her daughter.

Others followed and moved into the newly designed facility that volunteer contractors, architects, high school students, and a multitude of people with individual gifts had provided. Hope Haven became a struggling, but loving, community of eight single men, eight single women, and four families—so defined as having children. Hope Haven became the support system for people who had not had an adequate support system before. Medical assistance and counseling were provided. Classes in such areas as parenting, relationships, and spiritual awareness took place every night. GED classes and some college courses became a reality. Clients can live at Hope Haven for up to a year while choosing to turn their lives around.

Does it work? Yes, for those who want it to work, but it also provides a service beyond what it gives to the residents. Hope Haven provides a place—a safe place—where those who have a gift can give. Everyone has learned more about miracles, and who can put a price tag on that? Now Hope Haven has two great facilities. One building is for singles, and another building houses families. Literally hundreds have been through this program, and many lives have been changed. God's gifts still abound.

Looking back to Charles and the seed of the gift that was given to me, I am most grateful. I am grateful to God for letting me be a part of His gift of Hope Haven so I might better know how willing He is to work patiently and lovingly through His gifts to people like me.

Jackie Warmsley, May 2009
First Director, Abilene Hope Haven

Neglect not the gift that is in thee...
Timothy 4:14

The Gift

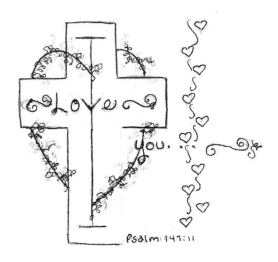

Psalm 147:11

Shadowy Cross by Sydney Senter McKinney

You can find the foot prints of God wherever
there is beauty, humility, justice, truth, love, And peace...
                                        Sri Sathya Sai Baba

The salvation of man is through love And in love...
                                        Viktor Frankl

If seeds in the black earth can turn into such beautiful roses, what might
not the heart of man become in its long journey toward the stars?
                                        G.K. Chesterson

Word Gift 1984:

Especially for You

By Lila Senter

The Word Gift was introduced to me by
A very special professor and person:
Caroline Couch Blair, McMurry University.
Word Gifts I have received are among my
most treasured possessions and memories.
They are also one of my favorite gifts to give.

As I pondered what Word Gift to share
that would have meaning for each of our
friends this Christmas, I remembered one
given us by our minister in the 1950s,
Dr. Norman Conner, First Christian Church, Abilene, Texas.
That is not so long ago, for the words are an original
Word Gift, centuries old—
given us by Him whose birthday we celebrate each
year with reverence, gratefulness, and joy.

Use it daily. Take time to capture the
Essence of the Christmas Spirit...
Through His words may you be
Lifted to new heights, and the
Spirit of Christmas be with you!

Amen!

In the beginning was the word, and the Word was with God, and the Word was God.

John 1

If eyes were made for seeing, then beauty is its own excuse for being.

Ralph Waldo Emerson

Calla Lilly by Alice Wright

The Lord's Prayer

Our Father which art in heaven,
Hallowed be thy name.
Thy kingdom come.
Thy will be done in earth
as it is in heaven.
Give us this day our daily bread.
And forgive us our debts,
as we forgive our debtors.
And lead us not into temptation,
but deliver us from evil:
For thine is the kingdom,
and the power, and the glory, forever.
Amen!

Matthew 6:9-13

Word Gift 1984:

Praying "The Lord's Prayer"

In his book *PRAYER*, Dr. George Buttrick offers these suggestions on how to use the Lord's Prayer as a guide:

Our Father, Who Art In Heaven,
"Help me to believe this day that there is a power to lift me up which is stronger than all the things that hold me down."
Hallowed Be Thy Name.
"Help me to be sensitive to what is beautiful, responsive to what is good, so that day by day I may grow more sure of the holiness of life in which I want to trust."
Thy Kingdom Come.
"Help me to be quick to see, and ready to encourage, whatsoever brings the better meaning of God into that which otherwise might be the common round of the uninspired day."
Thy Will Be Done On Earth As It Is In Heaven.
"Help me to believe that the ideals of the spirit are not a far-off dream, but a power to command my loyalty and direct my life here on our real earth."
Give Us This Day Our Daily Bread.
"Open the way for me to earn an honest living without anxiety; but let me never forget the needs of others, and make me want only that benefit for myself which will also be their gain."
And Forgive Us Our Trespasses, As We Forgive
Those Who Trespass Against Us.
"Make me sympathetic with the shortcomings of others, especially those I love; and keep me sternly watchful of my own. Let me never grow hard with unconscious cruelty of those who measure themselves by mean standards, and so think they have excelled. Keep my eyes lifted to the highest, so that I may be humbled, and seeing the failure of others may be forgiving, because I know how much there is of which I need to be forgiven."
And Lead Us Not Into Temptation, But Deliver Us From Evil.
"Let me not go carelessly this day within the reach of any evil I cannot resist, but if in the path of duty I must go where temptation is, give me strength of spirit to meet it without fear."
For Thine Is The Kingdom, And The Power,
And The Glory Forever and Ever.
"And so in my heart may I carry the knowledge that thy greatness is above men and around me, and that thy grace through Jesus Christ my master is Sufficient for all my needs."
Amen!

The Greatest Gift by Jane Milstead

Therefore the Lord himself will give you a sign; Behold, a virgin shall conceive, and bear a son, and shall call his name Immanuel.
Isaiah 7:14

Word Gift 2007:

God Came Down

By Lila Senter

Shh! Be still and listen—
Dwell in hushfulness.
Hear the sweet Spirit of God
Who gave to us the "why" of Christmas
And His love unceasing.

"It is time," God said, "for me to go down,
Be near my creation, and touch them."
So as prophets foretold so long ago—
"I'll begin in the town—Bethlehem."

He planted Himself in a virgin's womb,
Came to the world as you and as I.
Ah, the God Child born in wonderment,
Amazing love, and a baby's small cry.

O'erhead welcomed by an angel chorus,
A brilliant star, shepherds in the field—
Praises, starlit skylines, hallelujahs!
God's constant love was sealed.

God, manifested in Christ,
Came taking the burden of man's sin,
That he might know "joy beyond words"
And astonishing peace within.

Christmas, Lord Jesus, you gave to us—
O'er two thousand years we extol you!
Desiring "peace on earth", you brought the plans:
What Faith/Hope/Love in men's hearts can do!

You left us with your Holy Spirit, Lord,
And two lessons from Heaven above –
Love God with all of your heart, mind, and soul,
And to one's neighbors always show love.

Shh! Did you listen? Did you hear God come near?
Rejoice and tell Him,
"Happy Birthday! Merry Christmas, Jesu!"

Silent Night Holy Night of the Nativity by Sarabeth Clevenger

Love came down at Christmas; love all lovely, love divine; love was born at Christmas, stars and angels gave the sign.
                                                           Christina G. Rossetti

Praise ye him, sun and moon: praise him, all ye stars of light.
                                                           Psalm 148:3

Word Gift 1988:

OH "Silent Night" OH "Holy Night"

By Lila Senter

Amid the hum and the "hurry"
OF this CHRISTMAS season
Take time to be SILENT and
Think on the reason
For that long ago
Wondrous NIGHT
When a special STAR
In the sky shone bright
And GLORIFIED with
Angel Chorus a tiny BABE
Who all the difference
In this world has made.

Oh "Silent Night," Oh "Holy Night,"
May we see and know
Thy precious light;
A gift from HIM
To abide in men,
In EVERY heart that lets HIM in—
Ah, what changes from within!

Faith—Hope—Charity
But the greatest of these is charity.
1 Cor. 13:13

Hang a wish of love on your tree from us...

Mary and Baby Jesus by Ruth Jackson

Word Gift 1996:

Wrapped in a Manger

By Lila Senter

How they glitter! How they shine!
Christmas boxes,
yours and mine!

Now beribboned, tinseled too,
How they glow
For me—For you!

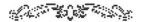

Then, there was no
Outward show.
The box was only a manger low.

Ah, but the gift—
Tiny baby…
And the Angels cry to all, "Come see!"

The very first
Christmas Gift—LOVE—
Was one supreme from God above.

Not wrapped in finery
Or outward show,
But a dear gift for the heart to know.

His name, JESUS—
Who said, "Love one another
As you would your sister, brother."

As we glorify this Christmas season,
May we always remember the reason…
From the manger He gave us
Faith, Hope, Love, these three,
But the greatest of these is LOVE/CHARITY.

Suggested reading: *The Christmas Box* by Richard Paul Evans

The LORD bless thee, and keep thee: The LORD make his face shine upon
thee, and be gracious unto thee: The LORD lift up his countenance upon
thee, and give thee peace.
Numbers 6:24-26

Señora Meditando by W.T. Nichols

In the sweetness of friendship let there be laughter,
For in the dew of little things the heart finds
Its morning and is refreshed.
Kahlil Gibran

Word Gift 1985:

Dear Friends

By Lila Senter

Between the first of the year
and its ending,
As we go through the
seasons once more,
We pause from the year's
occupations
And ponder our blessings galore.

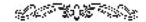

Among our most priceless blessings are friends,
both new and old—
Our close and very personal ones;
Those we have come to admire and appreciate
Through business associations;
Ones we have because we share a community,
And work together to make it the best;
Our neighbors and the joyous times of fellowship;
Our friends through church, and the
Common bond of worshiping together;
And those from the myriad other paths
Friends have entered our lives.

Spirits soar as we reflect on how each of you have
enriched, touched us in your own special way.
We wanted to take the
Opportunity
During this glorious, magical season, to say,
"We love you,
And thank you for your touch!"

Heavenly Star by Sydney McKinney

For you were sometimes darkness, but now
are ye light in the Lord:
Walk as children of light.
                                    Ephesians 5:8

When they had heard the king, they departed and lo, the star which
they saw in the east, went before them, til it come and
stood over where the young child was.
                                    Matthew 2:9

Word Gift 1995:

The Star

By Lila Senter

Lo! He shattered the darkness:
"Let there be light!"
He sprinkled the skies with infinite stars—
Behold the starry night!

Through eons stars led, enlightened man,
But man needed more to be whole.
He needed yet an inner light
To restore his yearning soul.

*...and lo, the star which they saw in the east went before them until it
came and stood over where the young child lay.*
Matthew 2:9

From the eternal stars God chose a special
One, this holy night to adorn.
Then He gave the ultimate gift of love—
Jesus Christ was born!

It's Christmas! Fill your heart with His
Spirit, precious gift from above.
Then share His promise and hope of
"Peace, Good Will toward Men," and
Most of all, LOVE.

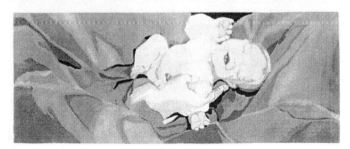

Nativity by Sarabeth Clevenger

When I consider thy heavens, the work of thy fingers, the moon and the stars, which thou hast ordained: what is man that thou are mindful of him? And the son of man, that thou visitest him?

Psalm 8:3-4

Word Gift 2006:

Christmas Is All About

By Sydney Senter McKinney and Lila Senter

The Infinite Cosmos, cradling heaven,
And oh, too, our Lord's abode.
God over all, in all—and from God
A tale wondrous does unfold.

Lo, the Word was in the beginning,
The Word with God—God the Word.
From the Word came the sweetest name
Creation, man, ever heard.

It is all about a prophecy,
A most miraculous birth.
God would come as His very own son,
Bringing light to this dark earth.

It is all about an angel's news,
The birth of a baby boy
Who left glory's throne for a stable
To fill hearts with His sweet joy.

It is all about a precious gift,
That forgiving gift of Grace—
Wrapped in a manger, hung on a cross,
For our sins He took our place.

It is all about gifts of selfless love
From a Man so good, so fine—
Who loved us enough to die for us,
Revealing love sublime.

It is all about His teaching us
To love and touch each other—
Giving our souls, our hearts, our time,
Reaching out to our brother.

It is all about Jesus' birthday—
God coming down from above,
Gifting us with power to shun evil, live peace—
It is the awesome gift of Love.

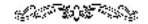

The Earth has grown old
With its burden of care
But at Christmas it always is young
The heart of the jewel burns lustrous and fair
And its soul full of music
Breaks the air
When the song of angels is sung.

Phillip Brooks,
American Episcopal Bishop,
Author of *Little Town of Bethlehem*
(1835-93)

Bethlehem Star by Sydney McKinney

Love Proclaimed by Linda Murphy

Christmas brings from us to you a story to be praised, about how the Spirit of Christmas enters a heart in strange and miraculous ways.
Lila Senter

Be not forgetful to entertain strangers: for thereby some have entertained angels unawares.
Hebrews 13:2

Word Gift 1987:

Incident on Fourth Street

By Norman Vincent Peale

One Christmas Eve, when I was a small boy, I was out with my father doing some last-minute errands on Fourth Street in Cincinnati. The packages I was carrying grew heavier with every step, and I could hardly wait to get home so Christmas could begin.

For this was the night when we three boys trimmed the tree, hung the stockings in front of the fireplace, and then the neighbors gathered around our piano for carols so lovely they made a lump in my throat.

It was while I was thinking these things that a hand touched mine. Beside me on the sidewalk stood a bleary-eyed, unshaven, old man, his other hand clutching a ragged cap in which lay a few pennies. I recoiled from the grimy fingers, turned my shoulder to him, and the old man crept away.

"You shouldn't treat a man that way, Norman," my father said.
"Aw, Dad, he's nothing but a bum."
"A bum?" my father said. "There is no such thing as a bum. He is a child of God. Maybe he hasn't made the most of himself, but he is God's beloved child just the same. Now I want you to go and give him this."

My father pulled out his pocketbook and handed me a dollar. This was a large sum for our family; most of our gifts to each other hadn't cost that much. "Now do exactly as I tell you. Go up to him, hand him this dollar, speak to him respectfully, and tell him you are giving him this dollar in the name of Christ."

"Oh, Dad!" I objected. "I couldn't say that!"
My father insisted, "Go and do as I tell you."
Reluctantly, I ran after the old man, caught up with him, and said, "Excuse me, sir, I give you this dollar in the name of Christ."
The old man looked at me in absolute surprise. Then a curious change came over his whole bearing, a new dignity into his manner. Graciously, with a sort of bow, he said, "And I thank you, young sir, in the name of Christ."
Suddenly the packages in my arms were lighter, the air was warmer, the very sidewalk was beautiful. No Christmas tree stood there, no carols filled the air, but all at once on Fourth Street, Christmas had begun.

May the Christmas Angel always touch hearts in new and wondrous ways! Amen!

Night Whispers by W.T. Nichols

That perfect time when one heart really listens and hears from another's heart.
Lila Senter

*Now the God of Hope fill you with all joy and peace in
believing, that ye may abound in hope...*
Romans 15:13

Word Gift 1989:

Happiness

Author Unknown

First,
An Eastern Tale—"Having created Heaven and Earth,
Flowers, Creatures, and Humankind, God created Happiness.
But where should happiness be?
In the deepest abyss, in the most luminous star,
In the darkest cave?
After a long reflection, our wise and eternal God decided:
I will hide happiness in the very heart of human beings.
There they will find it...if they look."

"Fear not: for behold, I bring you good tidings of great joy which shall be to all People."
Luke 2:10

Then,
Once upon a time, one holy starry night, a babe was born
And lo! So was CHRISTMAS...
Since then, the world, nor we, have ever been quite the same.
CHRISTMAS! Life everlasting, His gift!
CHRISTMAS! The Spirit of Love within each heart dwells,
preparing that special place for Hope, for Happiness.
CHRISTMAS! His gift which transcends all reason, and
somehow miraculously can bring about
"The Peace That Passeth Understanding."

May His love, hope, and joy be guests in your life
Wherever you are, now and always.
Lila Senter

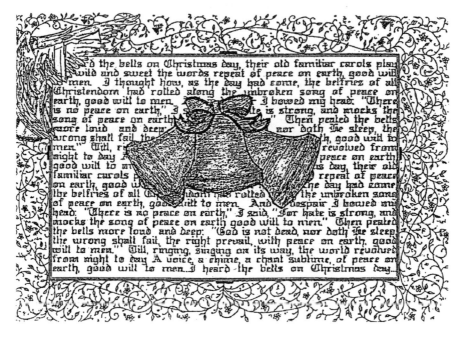

Bells by Sydney McKinney

The time draws near the birth of Christ:
The moon is hid; the night is still;
The Christmas bells from hill to hill
Answer each other in the mist.

Alfred Lord Tennyson

Sing unto the LORD, O ye saints of his,
And give thanks at the
Remembrance of his holiness.

Psalm 30:4

Word Gift 1994:

Christmas Bells

By Lila Senter

Bells! Bells! Bells! O, sweet Christmas Bells!
Hark to the news their chiming tells!
Companying the angel's lay,
Ringing gaily, they swing and sway
Resoundingly—as each rings and rings,
An angel in heaven wins its wings.
Then all together they peal, they sing,
Their great crescendos mightily bring
The Good News of Grace come to earth,
Praising the Christ Child's awesome birth.
A birth that changed world history,
Enlightened ancient mystery!
Christ came and darkness changed to light,
Stars in heaven glorified the night!

So
Join the angels and sing, sing, sing!
Echo the bell's rich ring, ring, ring!
Receive God's Gift, a wondrous Thing,
Christ in a manger, born a King!

O, hear and feel a Christmas song,
As bells strike their melodic dong,
And hope when'er you hear bells chime
Your heart is filled with love sublime!
Bells! Bells! Bells! O, sweet Christmas Bells!
Hark to the news their chiming tells!

Woman with Tea by Rosemary Suttle

Old-Fashioned Honey Cake:
A Zestful Holiday Treat

From *Uncle John's Bread Book* by John Braue

1 tsp. baking powder
1 tsp. baking soda
1 tsp. cinnamon
1 cup very strong Black Coffee (La. Style)
1 tsp. allspice
2 eggs, beaten
3/4 cup honey
1 cup sugar
1/2 cup salad oil
3 cups all-purpose flour, sifted
1/2 cup nuts, not chopped too finely (optional)

In a large mixing bowl, add oil to eggs, stirring. Add honey and coffee; then add sugar, gradually, plus all dry ingredients (sifted together), mixing thoroughly until colorful and smooth. Pour into a greased loaf pan and bake in a 325-degree oven for an hour.

Word Gift 1986:

Friendship Basket

By Lila Senter

It is time once again
For a holiday break…
From your busy schedule
Some quiet moments take.

SO
With honey-sweetened coffee cake
And hot, spicy tea,
Delight o'er your joys,
And know that we
Wish for you and yours
Blessings from above—-
Faith, Hope, and Charity,
But
The "Greatest is Love."

Accompanying these words a
Gift Basket filled with cake, tea,
Best Wishes and Love

Gifts of time and love are surely the basic ingredients of a truly Merry Christmas.
Peg Bracken

Be still, and know that I am God…
Psalm 46:10

Resounding Angels by Ginger Womack Taylor

And the angel said unto them, Fear not: for behold, I bring you tidings of great joy, which shall be to all people.
Luke 2:10

Word Gift 2000:

Angelic Ecstacy

By Lila Senter

Lo, Christ, our Savior King, was born that night,
The star above Bethlehem shone bright,
The heavens swelled with an angel chorus
Heralding God's awesome gift, just for us—

Angels sang so rapturously, majestically,
Their wings with joy shook vigorously,
Loosened their feathers, and to earth they fell,
A keepsake from Jesus—"All is well."

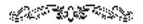

*Because He came, we have Christmas,
The gift of love for every heart!*

*For God so loved the world,
that He gave His only begotten Son...*
John 3:16

*...and she brought forth her first born son...
and laid Him in a manger...*
Luke 2:7

*...and suddenly there was with the angel a multitude of the Heavenly host
praising God and saying, Glory to God in the highest, and on earth Peace,
good will toward men.*
Luke 2:13-14

Peace On Earth by Tril Stratton

And the Holy Ghost descended in a bodily shape like a dove upon him, and a voice came from heaven, which said, Thou art my beloved Son; In thee I am well pleased."
Luke 3:22

Word Gift 1997:

The Dove

By Lila Senter

God looked down on His majestic earth,
Observed a world with little mirth.
Men's hearts were dark as is the night.
God said, "It is time! They need the Light."

Unto the world a King was born
To change His people so forlorn.
In a lowly manger in Bethlehem,
From heaven a chorus of seraphim,
And in the fields awed shepherds quake,
Rejoicing the difference Christ would make.

Hallelujah! Hallelujah! Jesus, His name!
The world would never ever be the same.
The babe was taken from where He laid
For purification rites—as Mary prayed,
God received their offering, a humble dove,
Yet a glorious symbol of His constant love.

Oh, whenever you see the dove melodic, so white,
Remember Jesus, who fills our hearts with light,
And as you see the dove take wing,
Open your hearts, the words of Jesus sing…
"Faith, Hope, Love, Peace, Joy"
Amen!
Gifts from the King born in Bethlehem.

Born In A Manger by Ginger Womack Taylor

And that he might make known the riches of his glory
on the vessels of mercy, which he had afore
prepared unto glory.

Romans 9:23

Word Gift 2004:

His Greatest Gift

By Lila Senter

Awesome! How Awesome!
In a world torn asunder,
Love dared to be born—
God's Gift...ultimate wonder!

Ancient world—chaos,
Strife, and morals gone astray;
Though good was alive,
It was oft hushed, like today.

Then near the temple
Of wicked Herod the King,
A precious babe's born
In a manger...One True King!

Oh, the risk God took
Was surely like no other.
He came, lowly birth,
Through a teenage mother.

His pomp, circumstance,
Were shepherds, radiant star,
Heaven's angel's voices
Exalting Christ from afar!

His crown was the moon,
Beaming stars, glowing sun.
He was God's promise,
"Love's Way"—Gift to everyone!

...so it came to pass, a babe was born
Unlike any other ever
...and it came to pass a King was born
Unlike any other ever
...He gave us Christmas, and changed
The world like no other ever. Amen!

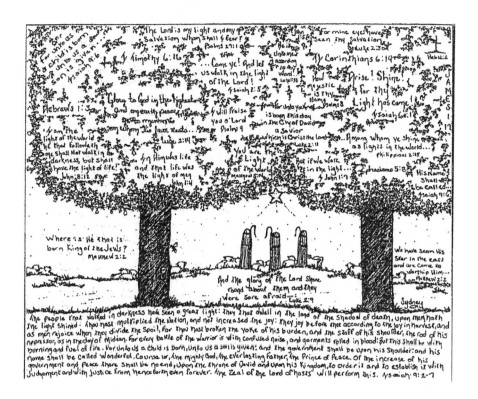

CHRISTmasTREE by Sydney McKinney

Then shall the King say unto them on his right hand, Come,
Ye blessed of my father, inherit the kingdom prepared for
you from the foundation of the world:
For I was a hungered, and you gave me meat: I was thirsty,
And you gave me drink: I was a stranger and you took me in:
Naked, and you clothed me: I was in prison and you came unto me.
Matthew 25:34-36

Verily I say unto you, inasmuch as ye have done it unto one of the least of
these my brethren, ye have done it unto me.
Matthew 25:40

Word Gift 1991:

CHRISTmas TREE

By Sydney Senter McKinney

We come bearing a special CHRISTmas TREE Adorned with HIS word & prophecy...A precious reminder of "why Christmas." May it come as the CHRIST CHILD came:

> *GENTLY...with the gift of HOPE*
> *PRAYERFULLY...with the gift of PEACE*
> *HUMBLY...with the gift of LOVE*
> *JOYFULLY...with the gift of LIFE.*
>   BJ Hoff

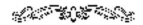

> *For CHRISTMAS Began In The Heart Of GOD*
> *And Is Complete Only When It Reaches The Heart Of Man.*
>   Author unknown

> *Finally, brethren, whatsoever things are true,*
> *Whatsoever things are honest,*
> *Whatsoever things are just,*
> *Whatsoever things are pure,*
> *Whatsoever things are lovely,*
> *Whatsoever things are of good report;*
> *If there be any virtue, and if there be any praise,*
> *Think on these things.*
>   Phillipians 4:8

Pensive by Jane Milstead

In everything give thanks: for this is the will of God in Christ Jesus concerning you.
1 Thessalonians 5:18

Word Gift 1999:

Reflection

By Lila Senter

For God So Loved The World
He Gave His Only Begotten Son...
John 3:16

Blessing us from His Kingdom above
With the everlasting gift of love
That Christmas might dwell in every heart;
And to each other this love impart
With the hope that strife would cease
And on earth, toward men, good will and peace.

Though lives overflow with much ado this season, there
comes a time to pause, reflect, and our abundant blessings
count—remembering even when sadness enters our lives,
and it will, He promises "joy will come in the morning," and
it does...We have counted our blessings, each and every
one, and want to take this moment in time to say thank
you, our friends, for touching our lives, each in your own
inimitable way! We thank you, and wish for you as we
say good-bye to this century, hello to the next:

You will never lose your sense of wonder. For it, alone, has the power to make
every day a holiday!
Leo Buscaglia

Horse and Baby by Bill Wright

Away in a manger, no crib for a bed,
The little Lord Jesus laid down his sweet head.
The stars in the sky looked down where he lay,
The little Lord Jesus asleep in the hay.
　　　　　　　　　　"Away In A Manger", 1885

Word Gift 1998:

The Heart of Christmas

By Lila Senter

What is Christmas? A glory to see!
God's restorative gift to you and me.
Christmas came to us when Love was born,
A babe's dear cry in the early morn.
From on high God gave to a needy earth
Love, sweet love, with Christ's holy birth...

For all to receive through an open Heart
Overflowing for you—then, to impart.
Agape love which is like no other
Asks simply: lose self, love one another.
If we will let love master, strife will cease.
Perhaps then, we all can know His blessed peace.

For we will see the cloud's silver lining,
Have the calm within for which we are pining,
Discover our candle shines even brighter
With burdens made so very much lighter.
Yes, Christ in our hearts, love fills each of our days.
Thank you, God, for Christmas, now and always.

There is a magnet in your heart that collects true friends. That magnet is unselfishness, thinking of others first.
Paramahansa Yogananda

For thou wilt light my candle; the Lord my God will enlighten my darkness.
Psalm 18:28

Three Kings by Billye Proctor Shaw

Now faith is the substance of things hoped for, the evidence of things not seen.
Hebrews 11:1

Word Gift 1993:

An Angel Story

By Lila Senter

Once upon a time infinitely old
A legend was born that yearns to be told.
It is one, perhaps, you would like to know,
This rare tale of an angel known as Snow.

Ah, read, imagine the Angel's story.
T'was a night of splendor, wondrous glory!
Into a world dark, his flock so forlorn,
A King in a lowly manger was born.

He came and cast, oh, such a lovely light
That heavenly, star-studded, snow-filled night—
Bringing everlasting hope, joy, sweet peace,
And a love that will never, ever cease.

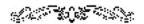

The Legend

Author Unknown

In a wintry land of the east, a little princess waited for
Her father to return from a journey. He sought a new
Savior King promised by God. As the girl knelt in the
Snow and prayed for her father's return, a beautiful
Angel appeared. "Your father is one of the three wise
men who have followed God's star safely to a manger
and will return with tidings of great joy."
No one believed the little girl's account of the angel's visit.
But months later, when her father returned with news of
the Baby Jesus, the princess led him to the place the Angel
had appeared. There, on the ground, while snow fell all
around and blanketed the countryside, one bare patch of
earth remained untouched by snow…
in the perfect shape of an ANGEL.

His Love by M.F. Robertson

A new commandment I give unto you, that ye love one another;
As I have loved you, that ye also love one another.
                                        John 13:34

Word Gift 2008:

Gift of Love

By Lila Senter

We thank you, O Lord, for Christmas,
A most beautiful time of the year.
We rejoice, sing praises, adore you
For such a gift, for love so dear.

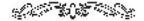

There was a time so long ago
When love incarnate walked among us.
God ventured to earth as His own Son,
A treasure most precious—Jesus!

Our world had a great need for Love,
Which comes from the heart, true and pure.
Pomp, Eros, Phileo—teeming, end...
Yet Agape alone does endure.

Christians thus heartened at Christmas,
Around the world touch and reach out.
For the love God revealed and gave us,
We pray we show what it's all about.

Let us keep God's plan now and ever:
Be honest, do good, be forgiving,
Be happy, be kind, and give our best.
May we give God's love while we're living!

Yes, we thank you, Lord, for Christmas,
The way it affects so many hearts,
And blesses us with awesome wonder,
This gift that your love imparts.

A Tale of Love Referred to as God's Wings

Author Unknown

After a forest fire, a park ranger found
a bird literally petrified in ashes, perched
statuesquely on the ground at the base of a tree. Somewhat
sickened by the eerie sight, he knocked over the bird with
a stick. When he gently struck it, three tiny chicks scurried
from under their dead mother's wings. The loving mother,
keenly aware of impending disaster, had carried her
offspring to the base of the tree and had gathered them
under her wings, instinctively knowing that the toxic
smoke would rise. She could have flown to safety
but had refused to abandon her babies. Then the
blaze had arrived and the heat had scorched
her small body; the mother had remained
steadfast. Because she had been willing
to die, those under the cover
of her wings would live.

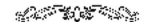

He shall cover thee with his feathers
And under His wings shalt thou trust.
Psalm 91:4

The Dove by Sydney McKinney

Anticipating the Wonder by Maggy Morford

But if we hope for that we see not, Then do we with patience wait for it.
Romans 8:25

Word Gift 1990:

Christmas

By Lila Senter

The sweetest most enduring gifts are those which come from the heart:

For God so loved the World that HE gave His only begotten son...
John 3:16

Who gave to us Christmas—
A gentle, magic time to
Quiet our souls and be reminded to:

C *heer someone with your smile.*
H *ug someone (minimum of five per day).*
R *emember to encourage someone.*
I *ncrease your knowledge of love.*
S *end someone a gift.*
T *hank someone.*
M *ail a love letter/thoughtful note to someone.*
A *ssure someone of your love.*
S *hare yourself; it's your most valuable gift.*
Leo Buscaglia

May you know Christmas wonder,
Feel its warmth, and share its love
Throughout this season and New Year!

Starbright by Sydney McKinney

This I recall to my mind, therefore have I hope. It is of the LORD's mercies that we are not consumed, because his compassions fail not. They are new every morning: great is thy faithfulness.
Lamentations 3:21-23

Word Gift 1992:

One Angelic Night

Lila Senter

"It Came Upon The Midnight Clear"
Stars exploded in God's heaven
Bringing new light to a darkened world.
Stars danced and twinkled across the sky
This "Silent Night, Holy Night"
Applauding an angelic choir...
"Hark The Herald Angels Sing,"
Glory! "Glory, to the newborn King!"
Christ The Savior! Hallelujah!
A message of renewed faith, eternal hope,
A new meaning of love—Christmas has come!
"Joy to the World!"

God then brought forth His special angels
Their numbers as awesome as stars in the sky...
Each star a celestial abode, harboring the
Guardian Angel given each of us—an angel
Who touches us in myriad, unexpected, and
Often unrecognizable ways, reminding us of
His constancy. Yes, "The First Noel" the
Angels did sing..."Angels We Have Heard on High",
Declaring: Miracles abound, we only need to see them!

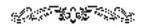

May your Christmas know a happy heart,
Moments of wonder,
And the kiss of your angel!

The Partridge Sings by Carie Hampton

Word Gift 2005:

Celebrate the Joy

By Lila Senter

Through music from ages past, and in the present, our
Lord and Savior touches our hearts, often lifting them to
Heights we have not dreamed. Yet, also, there is the
Music when our hearts meet His in merriment and joy—
With maybe even a hidden message.
"Partridge in a Pear Tree" is such a merry Christmas song—
But what else might it be saying?
England, 1558-1829—Religious practice for some was a crime:

So
A catechism song for the young was birthed,
Though religious, captured our Lord's mirth.

Ah, the Partridge, happy in the tree—
Jesus, lover of all humanity!
Two Turtle Doves—Old, and then a New Testament.
Three French Hens—Faith/Hope/Love for the heart's content.
Four Calling Birds—Gospels Mark, Luke, John, and Matthew.
Five Golden Rings—Torah, the Law to imbue.
Six Geese Laying—Six days of creation.
Seven Swans swimming—Holy Spirit's seven gifts of elation.
Eight Maids Milking—Beatitudes of high merit.
Nine Ladies Dancing—Fruits of the Holy Spirit.
Ten Lords Leaping—Commandments to live by.
Eleven Pipers Piping—Disciples faithful till they die.
Twelve Drummers Drumming—Apostles' creed,
Its points to remember, oh indeed.

Yes,
True love makes it all happen, for He enfolds us
With His loving care, puts His truth for us everywhere.
For thousands of years His Word has not been stilled long,
and ne'er will be, if we but remember the Partridge's Song.

The Gift by Nancy Capra

Word Gift 2003:

In The Beginning—Then Christmas
By Lila Senter

In the beginning—without form, empty and dark,
God's spirit hovered over this planet so stark...
By day seven, God painted, sculpted His chosen earth—
A ravishing, dazzling, brilliant land of worth.

Producing life teeming in water, on land, in sky—
Looking down from His supreme throne on high
He knew one more thing He must do by His Hand:
Yearning for love, in His image, He created man!

Ah, love, beauty—nakedness, no shame,
Until the deceiver—the one they would blame.
Alas! Now precious fellowship with God, and joy,
Find thorns in Eden from such ploy.

By way of Abraham, Moses, David, prophets all,
God sought to free His people from the dreadful fall,
Till the Old Testament ends with His last words spoken
Through the prophet Malachi—God's heart was broken!

His word was silent for four hundred years,
But God does not leave us with only our fears.
His love-hope-joy-peace endure forever!
Abandon his people? Oh, never! No, never!

So it was in a world of greed, idols, and power
God broke His silence and said, "Now is the hour."
The heavens exploded with glad tidings, joyful song,
The Good News for which man had waited so long.

THEN CHRISTMAS

Great joy o'er the birth of a babe, tiny thing—
Love embodied, Word incarnate, our Savior King!
Incomprehensible, awesome, God came down—Love to impart.
What does He ask of us? Only our heart!

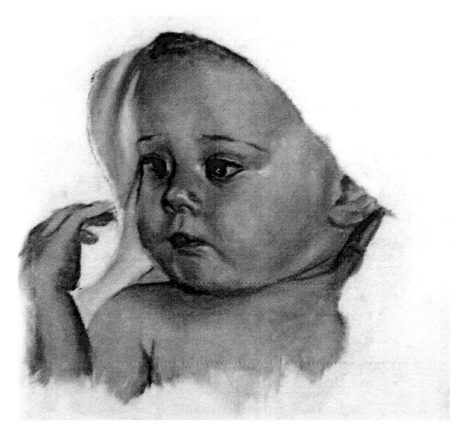

Baby Dear by Linda Murphy

Word Gift 2001:

The Child in Christmas

By Sydney Senter McKinney

God knew from the beginning
Christmas would be a special day.
It happened centuries ago.
He always planned it that way.

He brings out the child in Christmas,
a time for all to enjoy—
Precious wonder for all people
In this little baby boy.

The excitement of the moment
When his mother gave him birth—
Thoughts exploding in her heart,
The Savior to all the earth!

His first smile, first words, first steps,
Pre-planned to happen just that way,
To bring to us the reason
For this most awesome day.

His birth, His walk, His teachings
Mean nothing, nor the nail scars on each hand,
Had he not lived the truth, then died,
Only to live again!

How precious! How exciting,
That His birth of long ago
Is celebrated by us today,
And the Bible told us so!

The smiles on children's faces,
Grandchildren, those to come some day,
Can wake Christmas morn keeping
Jesus, who in a manger lay.

Presents, wreaths, and candy canes,
Chocolate, mistletoe, lights, and trees
Are symbols of celebrations to
The God of Eternity.

When thinking upon God this Christmas,
And the abundance of gifts we give,
Think upon the gift He gave—
Because of Him, we live!

A baby is God's opinion life should go on.
Carl Sandburg

Hannah Capra

Word Gift 2009:

It's Christmas

By Lila Senter

Tinsel glitters—
Red, gold, green—
Brightest lights
You've ever seen!
Stores are full,
Bells ring!
It's Christmas!

A child says,
"It's Santa Claus!"
His eyes dance—
Without a pause,
"I want a doll, a gun, or horn,"
Just because
It's Christmas!

Singing carols,
Stringing corn,
Kitchen aromas,
The house adorn,
Spreading joy,
Christ was born!
It's Christmas!

Nuts to crack,
The mistletoe,
Receiving cards—
Here's one from Joe!
Trim the tree
And watch it glow!
It's Christmas!

Loving, sharing,
You and I—
Feeling a special
Something lie
Within your heart.
As days go by,
Don't forget to
Remember why
It's Christmas!

So then faith cometh by hearing, And hearing by the Word of God.
Romans 10:17

Old Earth New Birth by Sarabeth Clevenger

Word Gift 2010:

The Gift of Light

By Lila Senter

It's Christmas! It's Christmas!
Happy Birthday, Lord—
And thank you, thank you—for LIGHT.

****

Light, a gift from the beginning
To light up the dark infinite void,
And, too, our remarkable Earth…
Sun, Moon, and Stars, glorious wonders,
Shining on us then, now, and always.

Yet, a Light like the world has never seen
Came when our Lord appeared—
Love personified, to light the souls of men.
A gift from Him for everyone—its home?
Our hearts, and you just invite him in.

Jesus, light of the world! Christ, who is God,
Took on flesh and dwelt among us
For a brief moment in time, that we might
Have fellowship with Him and
Fellowship with one another.

With His love in our hearts, no matter
How dark the night of life, His light brings back
The day. This light is everlasting, for as
He returned to Heaven's Throne
He anointed us with His Holy Spirit.

As the light is forever in our hearts, at Christmas
We are driven to share, AND
Love does explode across the world, near and far—
With multiple acts of generosity, compassion,
And the pouring out of treasure, talent, and time.

It's Christmas! God, Jesus, Holy Spirit—All in ONE!
With God in our hearts, there is hope in our hearts
That comes from His "light" and His "love."

✶✶✶✶✶✶✶✶✶✶✶✶✶✶✶✶✶✶✶✶✶✶✶✶✶✶✶✶✶✶

Then spake Jesus again unto them, saying, I am the light of the world: he that followeth me shall not walk in darkness, but shall have the light of life.
John 8:12

And God said, Let there be light: and there was light. And God saw the light, that it was good: and God divided the light from the darkness.
Genesis 1:3-4

The Mission by Alice Wright

"The Love of God is passionate. He pursues each of us Even when we know it not."

William Wordsworth

Lord's Prayer

Our Father which art in heaven, Hallowed be thy name.
Thy kingdom come. Thy will be done, as in heaven, so
in earth. Give us day by day our daily bread.
And forgive us our sins: for we also forgive everyone
That is indebted to us. And lead us not into temptation;,
but deliver us from evil. Amen.

Luke 11:2-4

Word Gift 2002:

...and Again, Especially For You, A Word Gift

By Lila Senter

Christmas Time!
I am still...considering a Word Gift for you
this year, and too, reflecting on this past
century and the amazing changes wrought.
Moving on, thinking about the new century
just beginning, we can only imagine the
marvels it will produce...
which returns my thoughts to Christmas,
dwelling on the marvel God produced,
so constant in our lives.

1984—Our first Word Gift to you!
It bears "recycling" as we journey the path
of this new century. It is His
Word Gift we carry in our heads and
hearts, which remains steadfast in our
souls though the world and life around us changes...
The Lord's Prayer!
Given to us from Jesus—Savior King—it is as
fresh, rich, and meaningful today as it
was yesterday.
As in ages past, with joy and devotion,
We celebrate His birthday
reminding us of his abiding love.

The Lord's Prayer

Our Father Which art in heaven, Hallowed be thy name.
Thy kingdom come. Thy will be done in earth as it is in heaven.
Give us this day our daily bread.
And forgive us our debts, as we forgive our debtors.
And lead us not into temptation, but deliver us from evil:
For thine is the kingdom, and the power, and the glory, forever.
Amen!

Matthew 6:9-13

Afterword

Abilene Hope Haven celebrated fifteen years of service to individuals and families who experience homelessness in June 2009. More than 1,800 people have entered the program since we accepted our first resident. Hope Haven offers people a place to live up to one year while they work to remedy their homeless situation. We do more than just offer people shelter, though. Abilene Hope Haven provides food, clothing, transportation, and supportive services as well. The goal for all our residents is to become self-sufficient, responsible, and productive members of our community.

We offer a safe and stable living environment. Our residents do not have to worry about where they will spend the night. Hope Haven becomes a home they can depend on and trust to be here at the end of their day. Structure and support are built into the program; life routines and daily habits are good practices that help all of us live well. The program provides life-skill training through education classes taught by community volunteers. Learning new ways to handle money or parent, for example, can often point a resident to a more positive future. Our residents are given an opportunity for counseling, if they desire the assistance. Finally, we want our residents to acquire new relationships in their lives so they have a broader base of support when they complete the program and move on in life.

Since the day Abilene Hope Haven opened its doors, the foundational principle remains the same: provide a supportive environment where people are given an opportunity to change the way they have been living. And often they will. The hard work of change is not something we can do for folks. But we can hold them up in hope and prayer while they make changes that make a better future possible.

On behalf of Abilene Hope Haven, I want to thank Lila Senter for supporting this program in many ways through the years. This book is the outcome of her dreaming of new ways to help secure the future of this nonprofit—a future secured not for the sake of the organization, but for the sake of the next individual or family who wants to escape homelessness.

Randy Halstead,
Executive Director

In March 2010, our single residents moved out of the original Abilene Hope Haven building and into a scattered site program. This change to our single adult program allows residents more independence while they work toward their goals of selfsufficiency.

These single residents are now living in a roommate situation in local apartments. Abilene Hope Haven provides all basic needs, including: shelter, food, case management, transportation & life skills to these individuals.

Our family residents continue to reside at our family facility, located at 801 S. Treadaway.

In June 2010, I was blessed with the opportunity to become the Executive Director of Abilene Hope Haven. Our transitional housing program for single individuals and families cosntinues to improve lives in the Abilene community on a daily basis. This program would not be possible without the support of the community and wonderful volunteers. We are grateful to Lila Senter for continuing to support Abilene Hope

Haven's future through our endowment fund. With your support, we are continuing to strive toward our mission to "cure homelessness, one person at a time."

Alana Jeter, Executive Director
Abilene Hope Haven, Inc.

Hope
Is the thing with
Feathers
That perches in the
Soul
And sings the tune
Without the words
And
Never stops at all

Emily Dickenson

This little book, first inspired by
A hope for an endowment fund
begun for Abilene HOPE HAVEN,
with All contributions going toward
this goal, succeeded. It has begun!
We now hope to expand the hope and
goal of THE GIFT.
ALL net proceeds will go to:
Community Foundation Abilene/Grant
Distribution/Senter Family Fund...
to aid not only the endowment fund
but the many and variable needs of
Abilene HOPE HAVEN.
Get and/or Give THE GIFT,
Be assured, it keeps on Giving!

Community Foundation Abilene
Senter Family Fund
P.O. Box 1001
Abilene, TX 79604

Hope Angel by Bill Wright

Artist and Photographer Contacts

Saraphim V by Sarabeth Clevenger

Capra, Hannah	Twig and Willow 1133 N. 2nd St. Abilene, TX 79601
Capra, Nancy	Twig and Willow 1133 N. 2nd St. Abilene, TX 79601
Clevenger, Sarabeth	franclev@suddenlink.net (325) 676-3187
Milstead, Jane	(325) 673-4851 (325) 829-3430
Nichols, W.T.	gnwtnichols@aol.com (325) 793-2585
Robertson, M.F.	mfr1934@yahoo.com
Stratton, Tril	bill-tril@sbcglobal.net
Taylor, Ginger Womack	gwtaylor1@suddenlink.net
Wright, Alice	alicewright@wrightworld.com
Wright, Bill	billwright@wrightworld.com

Origins of Christmas Songs

The following familiar Christmas Songs inspired the Word Gift
"One Angelic Night"

1. "It Came Upon the Midnight Clear" (1849): Words, Edmund Hamilton Sears; Music, Richard Storrs Willis
2. "Silent Night Holy Night" (1816): Words, Joseph Mohr; Melody, Franz Xaver Gruber
3. "Hark! The Herald Angels Sing" (1739): Words, Charles Wesley
4. "Joy to the World" (1719): Words, Isaac Watts; Melody, Lowell Mason
5. "The First Noel": Unknown in origin, but believed to be English and date back to sixteenth century
6. "Angels We Have Heard on High": Based on a French Carol known as *Les Anges dans nos Compagnes* (Angels in our Countryside). Common English version translated in 1862 by James Chadwick

Notes

Page 4   Word Gift 1984: "Praying The Lord's Prayer" by Dr.
             George Buttrick, from his book, *Prayer*. Permission to use
             from Dr. David Butrick, Buffington Professor of
             Homiletics and Liturgics, Emeritus, Vanderbilt.

Page 20   Word Gift 1987: "Incident On Fourth Street" by Norman
             Vincent Peale. Reprinted with permission from
             Guideposts. Copyright 1984 by Guideposts. All rights
             reserved.

Page 25   Word Gift 1986: Recipe from my brother-in-law, John
             Braue, now deceased. His family, from Germany, were
             master bakers. He made a book of his family's recipes in
             1961. Laced with family stories, it is a fun read.

Page 46   Word Gift 1990: "CHRISTMAS"—each letter a gift we
             each may give. Telephone conversation Leo Buscaglia
             Foundation, Palos Verdes Estates, CA. Oral permission
             from Jeff to use special words from a Christmas card sent
             to us from Leo Buscaglia.

Page 48   Word Gift 1992: "One Angelic Night" was inspired by the
             following familiar Christmas Carols: "It Came Upon the
             Midnight Clear", "Silent Night, Holy Night", "Hark! The
             Herald Angels Sing", "Joy to the World", "The First Noel",
             and "Angels We Have Heard on High".

Page 50   Word Gift 2005: Sevenfold Gifts of the Holy Spirit: Isaiah
             11:1-3; Beatitudes: Matthew 5:3-11; Fruits of the Holy
             Spirit: Galatians 5:22; Ten Commandments: Exodus 20:3-
             16/Deuteronomy 5:6-21; Disciples: Peter, Andrew, James,
             John, Philip, Bartholomew, Matthew, Thomas, James the
             Less, Simon, Jude

Page 55   Word Gift 2009: "It's Christmas" was written in 1968 for
             our children—Scott, Steve, and Sydney—to encourage
             their interest and joy in reading poetry.